POSITIVE MENTAL
gratitude

QUOTES AND AFFIRMATIONS
TO HELP YOU LOOK ON THE
BRIGHT SIDE OF LIFE

summersdale

POSITIVE MENTAL GRATITUDE

Compiled by Jess Zahra

An Hachette UK Company
www.hachette.co.uk

Summersdale Publishers Ltd
Part of Octopus Publishing Group Limited
Carmelite House
50 Victoria Embankment
LONDON
EC4Y 0DZ
UK

www.summersdale.com

Printed and bound in Poland

ISBN: 978-1-80007-836-9

Substantial discounts on bulk quantities of Summersdale books are available to corporations, professional associations and other organizations. For details contact general enquiries: telephone: +44 (0) 1243 771107 or email: enquiries@summersdale.com.

To...........................

From.......................

Gratitude is a
powerful catalyst
for happiness.
It's the spark that
lights a fire of
joy in your soul.

AMY COLLETTE

CARRY OUT A RANDOM ACT OF KINDNESS, WITH NO EXPECTATION OF REWARD, SAFE IN THE KNOWLEDGE THAT ONE DAY SOMEONE MIGHT DO THE SAME FOR YOU.

Diana, Princess of Wales

EVERY
DAY IS
a gift

APPRECIATION IS
A WONDERFUL
THING. IT MAKES
WHAT IS EXCELLENT
IN OTHERS BELONG
TO US AS WELL.

Voltaire

NO MATTER
WHAT HAPPENS
IN LIFE, BE
GOOD TO
PEOPLE. BEING
GOOD TO PEOPLE
IS A WONDERFUL
LEGACY TO
LEAVE BEHIND.

Taylor Swift

No one ever damaged their eyesight by looking on the bright side

Nothing to me feels as good as laughing incredibly hard.

STEVE CARELL

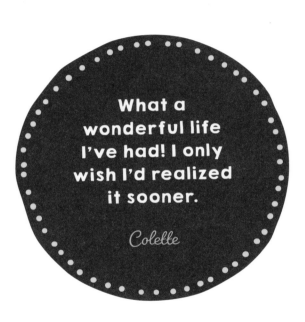

What a
wonderful life
I've had! I only
wish I'd realized
it sooner.

Colette

THERE ARE TWO WAYS
OF SPREADING LIGHT:
TO BE THE CANDLE,
OR THE MIRROR
THAT REFLECTS IT.

Edith Wharton

POSITIVITY
IS THE SECRET
TO HAPPINESS

The best and most
beautiful things
in the world
cannot be seen
or even touched.
They must be felt
with the heart.

HELEN KELLER

Turn your face to the sun and the shadows will fall behind you.

MĀORI PROVERB

Gratitude is riches.

Doris Day

Don't count
the days... make
the days count

It ain't no use putting up your umbrella till it rains.

ALICE HEGAN RICE

SOMETIMES
IT TAKES ONLY
ONE ACT OF
KINDNESS
AND CARING
TO CHANGE A
PERSON'S LIFE.

Jackie Chan

BAD EXPERIENCES
ARE LESSONS,
NOT FAILURES

Gratitude turns what we have into enough.

ANONYMOUS

OPTIMISM IS A
HAPPINESS MAGNET.
IF YOU STAY POSITIVE,
GOOD THINGS AND
GOOD PEOPLE WILL
BE DRAWN TO YOU.

Mary Lou Retton

THERE'S ALWAYS TOMORROW AND IT ALWAYS GETS BETTER!

Ariana Grande

You don't need a
reason to be happy -
choose to be happy!

AS WE EXPRESS
OUR GRATITUDE,
WE MUST NEVER
FORGET THAT
THE HIGHEST
APPRECIATION IS
NOT TO UTTER
WORDS, BUT TO
LIVE BY THEM.

John F. Kennedy

This is a
wonderful day.
I've never seen
this one before.

MAYA ANGELOU

GRATITUDE
IS THE BEST
attitude

If the only prayer
you said in your
whole life was
thank you, that
would suffice.

MEISTER ECKHART

PRACTISE RANDOM
KINDNESS AND
SENSELESS ACTS
OF BEAUTY.

Anne Herbert

"Enough"
is a feast.

Buddhist proverb

BELIEVE
IN MAGIC
AND YOU
WILL FIND IT

Whoever is happy will make others happy too.

ANNE FRANK

LET'S KEEP
LIFTING EACH
OTHER UP.

Lauren Graham

When things change inside you, they change around you

TODAY, FILL
YOUR CUP
OF LIFE WITH
SUNSHINE
AND LAUGHTER.

Dodinsky

YOU NEVER
LOSE BY
LOVING.
YOU ALWAYS
LOSE BY
HOLDING BACK.

Barbara De Angelis

Gratitude is not
only the greatest
of virtues, but the
parent of all others.

CICERO

WHEN YOU
FOCUS ON
THE GOOD,
THE GOOD
GETS BETTER

REMEMBER, HOPE
IS A GOOD THING,
MAYBE THE BEST OF
THINGS, AND NO GOOD
THING EVER DIES.

Stephen King

WHEN WE FOCUS
ON OUR GRATITUDE,
THE TIDE OF
DISAPPOINTMENT GOES
OUT AND THE TIDE
OF LOVE RUSHES IN.

Kristin Armstrong

Say good words,
think good things,
do good deeds

GRATITUDE MAKES
SENSE OF OUR PAST,
BRINGS PEACE FOR
TODAY, AND CREATES A
VISION FOR TOMORROW.

Melody Beattie

I KNOW THE
SUN WILL
RISE IN THE
MORNING,
THAT THERE IS
A LIGHT AT
THE END OF
EVERY TUNNEL.

Michael Morpurgo

A gentle word,
a kind look, a good-
natured smile can
work wonders and
accomplish miracles.

WILLIAM HAZLITT

YOUR LIFE IS
A PIECE OF ART
– IT DESERVES
TO BE ENJOYED

REMEMBER
THERE'S NO
SUCH THING
AS A SMALL ACT
OF KINDNESS.
EVERY ACT
CREATES A
RIPPLE WITH NO
LOGICAL END.

Scott Adams

LIFE IS SO MUCH
BIGGER, GRANDER,
HIGHER, AND WIDER
THAN WE ALLOW
OURSELVES TO THINK.

Queen Latifah

INHALE
LOVE,
EXHALE
gratitude

Be silly. Be kind.
Be weird.
There's no time for
anything else.

NANEA HOFFMAN

Forever is
composed
of nows.

Emily Dickinson

THE MOST
IMPORTANT
THING IS TO
ENJOY YOUR
LIFE, TO BE
HAPPY. IT'S ALL
THAT MATTERS.

Audrey Hepburn

Kindness is like snow —
it beautifies
everything it covers.

KAHLIL GIBRAN

THE GIFTS
OF CARING,
ATTENTION,
AFFECTION,
APPRECIATION,
AND LOVE
ARE SOME
OF THE MOST
PRECIOUS GIFTS
YOU CAN GIVE.

Deepak Chopra

Sometimes when
we are generous
in small, barely
detectable ways it
can change someone
else's life forever.

MARGARET CHO

GOOD ENERGY IS
contagious

LIFE IS TOUGH;
AND IF YOU HAVE
THE ABILITY TO LAUGH
AT IT, YOU HAVE THE
ABILITY TO ENJOY IT.

Salma Hayek

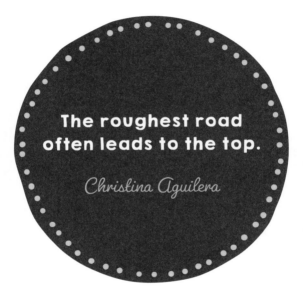

The roughest road
often leads to the top.

Christina Aguilera

BE THANKFUL FOR
WHAT YOU HAVE;
YOU'LL END UP
HAVING MORE.

Oprah Winfrey

THE IMPORTANT
THING IS NOT
HOW MANY
YEARS IN YOUR
LIFE, BUT HOW
MUCH LIFE IN
YOUR YEARS!

Edward Stieglitz

Let's practise motivation and love, not discrimination and hate.

ZENDAYA

The sun is always
shining somewhere
in the world

HAPPINESS
LOOKS
GORGEOUS
ON YOU

Life is either a daring adventure or nothing.

Helen Keller

THE ROOT OF JOY IS GRATEFULNESS.

David Steindl-Rast

Gratitude will shift you to a higher frequency, and you will attract much better things.

RHONDA BYRNE

Who cares about winning or losing? Life is more fun when taking part

When life looks like
it's falling apart,
it may just be
falling into place.

BEVERLY SOLOMON

If things go wrong,
don't go with them.

Roger Babson

GRATITUDE
HELPS YOU FALL
IN LOVE WITH
THE LIFE YOU
ALREADY HAVE

LOVE AND
KINDNESS ARE
NEVER WASTED.
THEY ALWAYS
MAKE A
DIFFERENCE.

Barbara De Angelis

BE HEALTHY AND TAKE
CARE OF YOURSELF,
BUT BE HAPPY WITH
THE BEAUTIFUL THINGS
THAT MAKE YOU, YOU.

Beyoncé

THE MORE
GRATEFUL I AM,
THE MORE
BEAUTY I SEE.

Mary Davis

A BEAUTIFUL
DAY BEGINS WITH
A BEAUTIFUL
MINDSET

DO NOT SPOIL
WHAT YOU HAVE
BY DESIRING
WHAT YOU HAVE
NOT; REMEMBER
THAT WHAT YOU
NOW HAVE WAS
ONCE AMONG THE
THINGS YOU
ONLY HOPED FOR.

Epicurus

The most important
thing you can do
for another person
is to validate
their existence.

MARIE FORLEO

HAPPINESS
IS AN
inside job

THE POWER OF
FINDING BEAUTY IN
THE HUMBLEST THINGS
MAKES HOME HAPPY
AND LIFE LOVELY.

Louisa May Alcott

The fragrance always stays in the hand that gives the rose.

GEORGE WILLIAM CURTIS

KINDNESS IS A
LANGUAGE WHICH
THE DEAF CAN
HEAR AND THE
BLIND CAN SEE.

Anonymous

A GRATEFUL
HEART IS
A MAGNET
FOR JOY

THE MORE
YOU EXPRESS
GRATITUDE FOR
WHAT YOU HAVE,
THE MORE LIKELY
YOU WILL HAVE
EVEN MORE
TO EXPRESS
GRATITUDE FOR.

Zig Ziglar

ASK YOURSELF:
HAVE YOU
BEEN KIND
TODAY? MAKE
KINDNESS YOUR
DAILY MODUS
OPERANDI AND
CHANGE YOUR
WORLD.

Annie Lennox

Expect nothing,
appreciate
everything

It's never too late
– never too late to
start over, never too
late to be happy.

JANE FONDA

CHANGE YOUR
THOUGHTS AND
YOU CHANGE
YOUR WORLD.

Norman Vincent Peale

For every minute you are angry you lose 60 seconds of happiness.

RALPH WALDO EMERSON

GRATITUDE CHANGES *everything*

Love and kindness
go hand in hand.

Marian Keyes

The little things? The little moments? They aren't little.

JON KABAT-ZINN

HAPPY MIND,
HAPPY LIFE

DELETE
THE NEGATIVE;
ACCENTUATE
THE POSITIVE!

Donna Karan

Be in love with your life. Every detail of it.

Jack Kerouac

The smallest act
of kindness is
worth more than
the grandest intention.

OSCAR WILDE

I URGE YOU TO
PLEASE NOTICE
WHEN YOU ARE
HAPPY, AND
EXCLAIM OR
MURMUR OR THINK
AT SOME POINT,
"IF THIS ISN'T
NICE, I DON'T
KNOW WHAT IS."

Kurt Vonnegut

I've been searching
for ways to heal
myself, and I've
found that kindness
is the best way.

LADY GAGA

SOMETIMES,
THE SMALLEST
THINGS TAKE UP
THE MOST ROOM
IN YOUR HEART.

A. A. Milne

Bad vibes don't go
with your outfit

We often take for granted the very things that most deserve our gratitude.

CYNTHIA OZICK

THE TRUE SECRET OF
HAPPINESS LIES IN
TAKING A GENUINE
INTEREST IN ALL THE
DETAILS OF DAILY LIFE.

William Morris

YOU HAVE TO BELIEVE
IN YOURSELF WHEN
NO ONE ELSE DOES
– THAT MAKES YOU A
WINNER RIGHT THERE.

Venus Williams

CELEBRATE
YOUR VICTORIES,
NO MATTER
HOW SMALL

JOY IS WHAT
HAPPENS TO
US WHEN
WE ALLOW
OURSELVES TO
RECOGNIZE HOW
GOOD THINGS
REALLY ARE.

Marianne Williamson

NO ACT OF
KINDNESS,
HOWEVER
SMALL,
IS EVER
WASTED.

Aesop

KEEP HOPE IN *your heart*

The trick is to
enjoy life. Don't
wish away your
days, waiting for
better ones ahead.

MARJORIE PAY HINCKLEY

Life should not
only be lived,
it should be
celebrated.

OSHO

I WANT YOU TO KNOW
THAT YOU WOKE UP
THIS MORNING, AND
THAT'S A BLESSING.
I WANT YOU TO KNOW
THE SUN IS SHINING
SOMEWHERE... EVEN
IF IT'S RAINING, IT'S
CLEANSING YOU –
IT'S A BLESSING.

Lizzo

Inside every setback
hides opportunity

MAY YOU NEVER BE
SO BUSY LOOKING
FOR YOUR POT OF
GOLD THAT YOU MISS
OUT ON APPRECIATING
YOUR RAINBOW.

Karen Salmansohn

IT'S THE
CHOICE.
YOU HAVE TO
WAKE UP EVERY
DAY AND SAY,
"THERE'S NO
REASON TODAY
CAN'T BE THE
BEST DAY OF
MY LIFE."

Blake Lively

POSITIVE
ACTIONS LEAD
TO POSITIVE
RESULTS

COMPASSION
ISN'T ABOUT
SOLUTIONS.
IT'S ABOUT
GIVING ALL
THE LOVE THAT
YOU'VE GOT.

Cheryl Strayed

What wisdom can you find that is greater than kindness?

Jean Jacques Rousseau

It's not about what you have or even what you've accomplished... It's about who you've lifted up, who you've made better. It's about what you've given back.

DENZEL WASHINGTON

Live for the
moments you can't
put into words

WE CAN ALWAYS USE
MORE KINDNESS IN
OUR LIVES, BUT I
THINK RIGHT NOW IS
A REALLY GOOD TIME
TO BE REMINDED OF
MAYBE SHARPENING
OUR KINDNESS SKILLS.

Julia Roberts

Kindness is the sunshine in which virtue grows.

ROBERT G. INGERSOLL

EVERY DAY IS A

second chance

GRATITUDE IS THE
CLOSEST THING TO
BEAUTY MANIFESTED
IN AN EMOTION.

Mindy Kaling

WE LEARNED
ABOUT
GRATITUDE
AND HUMILITY –
THAT SO MANY
PEOPLE HAD A
HAND IN OUR
SUCCESS.

Michelle Obama

The struggle ends
when gratitude
begins.

Neale Donald Walsch

WE RISE
BY LIFTING
others

WHEN YOU ARISE
IN THE MORNING,
THINK OF WHAT
A PRECIOUS
PRIVILEGE IT
IS TO BE ALIVE –
TO BREATHE,
TO THINK,
TO ENJOY,
TO LOVE.

Marcus Aurelius

Acknowledging the
good that you already
have in your life is
the foundation for
all abundance.

ECKHART TOLLE

STAY SUNNY ON
THE OUTSIDE
AND WARM ON
THE INSIDE

I CAN NO OTHER
ANSWER MAKE
BUT THANKS,
AND THANKS,
AND EVER
THANKS.

William Shakespeare

GRATITUDE OPENS
THE DOOR TO... THE
POWER, THE WISDOM,
THE CREATIVITY OF
THE UNIVERSE. YOU
OPEN THE DOOR
THROUGH GRATITUDE.

Deepak Chopra

BE PRESENT IN ALL
THINGS AND THANKFUL
FOR ALL THINGS.

Maya Angelou

Change starts
in your thoughts

A TIME WHEN
WE HAVE TO
SHED OUR FEAR
AND GIVE HOPE
TO EACH OTHER.
THAT TIME
IS NOW.

Wangari Maathai

I am happy because
I'm grateful. I choose
to be grateful. That
gratitude allows
me to be happy.

WILL ARNETT

START AND END
EACH DAY WITH
A POSITIVE
THOUGHT

If you see someone without a smile, give them one of yours.

DOLLY PARTON

A SINGLE ACT OF
KINDNESS THROWS
OUT ROOTS IN ALL
DIRECTIONS, AND THE
ROOTS SPRING UP AND
MAKE NEW TREES.

Amelia Earhart

Always laugh when you can. It is cheap medicine.

Lord Byron

Positive mind,
positive vibes,
positive life

GRATITUDE IS THE
WINE FOR THE SOUL.
GO ON. GET DRUNK.

Rumi

DON'T LET ANYONE STEAL YA JOY!

Missy Elliot

ALL GOOD
THINGS COME
FROM GRATITUDE

IN THE
DARK TIMES,
IF YOU HAVE
SOMETHING
TO HOLD ON
TO, WHICH
IS YOURSELF,
YOU'LL SURVIVE.

Whoopi Goldberg

Be driven, be focused,
but enjoy every
moment, because it
only happens once.

ALICIA KEYS

STRIVE TO FIND
THINGS TO BE
THANKFUL FOR,
AND JUST LOOK
FOR THE GOOD IN
WHO YOU ARE.

Bethany Hamilton

You are always in
the right place at
the right time

I thank everything,
because everything
teaches me
something.

Maxime Lagacé

FOR ME, EVERY HOUR
IS GRACE. AND I FEEL
GRATITUDE IN MY
HEART EACH TIME
I CAN MEET SOMEONE
AND LOOK AT HIS
OR HER SMILE.

Elie Wiesel

BE THE ENERGY
YOU WANT
TO ATTRACT

HAPPINESS IS
LETTING GO OF
WHAT YOU THINK
YOUR LIFE IS
SUPPOSED TO
LOOK LIKE AND
CELEBRATING IT
FOR EVERYTHING
THAT IT IS.

Mandy Hale

TRUE BEAUTY
IS BORN
THROUGH OUR
ACTIONS AND
ASPIRATIONS
AND IN THE
KINDNESS
WE OFFER
TO OTHERS.

Alek Wek

Look at the sky:
that is for you.
Look at each
person's face as
you pass them on
the street: those
faces are for you.

MIRANDA JULY

Unexpected twists
can add spice to life

EVEN IN THE
CHAOS OF EVERYDAY
LIFE, MOMENTS OF
GRATITUDE REMIND
US TO HOLD ON TO
THE GOOD THINGS.

Brit Morin

COMPASSION IS
CONTAGIOUS. EVERY
MOMENT WE CHOOSE
COMPASSION, WE
MOVE TOWARD A
BETTER WORLD.

Amit Ray

I have found that
if you love life,
life will love you back.

ARTHUR RUBINSTEIN

APPRECIATION
CAN MAKE A DAY
– EVEN CHANGE
A LIFE. YOUR
WILLINGNESS
TO PUT IT
INTO WORDS
IS ALL THAT
IS NECESSARY.

Margaret Cousins

REFUSE TO TAKE
ANY SINGLE DAY
FOR GRANTED

When I started counting my blessings, my whole life turned around.

Willie Nelson

POSITIVE MENTAL gratitude!

365 Days of Kindness

Vicki Vrint

Hardback

978-1-80007-100-1

This little book will help you find time every day for small acts of kindness and love. With innovative tips and a collection of inspiring quotations, it will be your guide to spreading goodwill and gratitude all year round.

Positivity for Every Day

Hardback

978-1-78783-651-8

Sometimes a positive outlook is all we need to help us see the sun behind the clouds. With inspiring quotations and simple tips, this little book will show you how to look on the bright side and achieve a more balanced attitude to life.

If you're interested in finding out more about our books, find us on Facebook at **Summersdale Publishers**, on Twitter at **@Summersdale** and on Instagram at **@summersdalebooks**

www.summersdale.com

Image credits

Stars, dots and rainbow © avian/Shutterstock.com